BEFORE YOU BEGIN...

Make sure to download the FREE audio program for this book which comes with your purchase! Just go to

www.slangman.com/audio

then look for your book and enter this code:

E2J23JEFJPBS

GOLDILOCKS and the 3 BEARS

Book Design
and Production:
Slangman Publishing.

Written by: David Burke
Copy Editor: Julie Bobrick
Illustrated by: "Migs!" Sandoval
Translator: Mariko Bird

Copyright © 2017 by David Burke

Email: info@heywordy.com
Website: www.heywordy.com

Hey Wordy! and all related characters and elements are © and trademarks of Hey Wordy, LLC.

Published by Slangman Publishing. Slangman is a registered trademark of David Burke. All rights reserved. Reproduction or translation of any part of this work beyond that permitted by section 107 or 108 of the 1976 United States Copyright Act without the permission of the copyright owner is unlawful. Requests for permission or further information should be addressed to the Permissions Department, Slangman Publishing. This publication is designed to provide accurate and authoritative information in regard to the subject matter covered. The persons, entities and events in this book are fictitious. Any similarities with actual persons or entities, past and present, are purely coincidental.

ISBN13: 978-1-891888-55-7

Printed in the U.S.A.

Meet the Author
David Burke

Creator and star of the children's TV show, *Hey Wordy!*, David Burke has been single-handedly revolutionizing the foreign language-learning movement worldwide.

In addition to being a performer of boundless energy and enthusiasm, David speaks seven languages. A successful author and entrepreneur, he has built a thriving international publishing company featuring over 100 books he has written for teen/adults & children. His books have won publishing awards and have sold more than one million copies. David's Street Speak™ and Biz Speak™ series of books and audio programs are used around the world by government agencies, leading universities and major corporations.

Since age 4, David has been a classically trained pianist and uses his musical gifts to compose and perform original songs for his TV series, *Hey Wordy!* which introduces children to foreign languages and cultures through music, animation, and magical adventures. He has also composed, orchestrated, and performed all the music in the audio programs for each of these books.

David's engaging and charismatic persona became a fixture on broadcast entertainment channels around the world, such as CNN and the BBC. David and his work have been highlighted in many major publications, including The Los Angeles Times, The Chicago Tribune and The Christian Science Monitor.

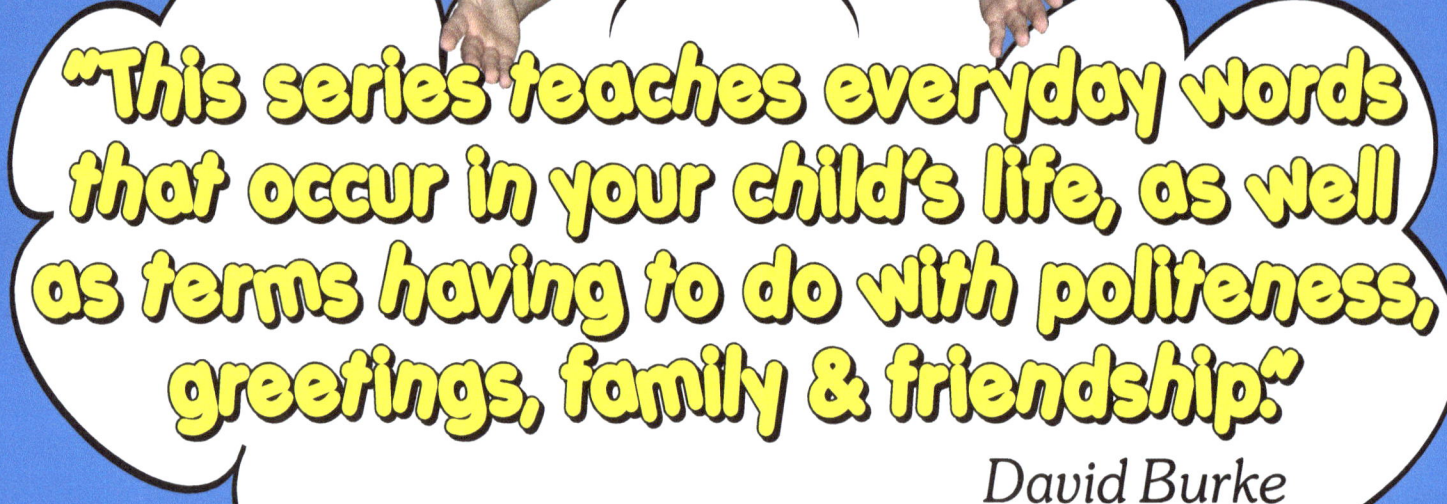

"This series teaches everyday words that occur in your child's life, as well as terms having to do with politeness, greetings, family & friendship."

David Burke

Japanese vocabulary taught:

atsui=hot
beddo=bed
bo'oru=bowl
cheesana=little
doa=door
eechee=one
eesu=chair
katai=hard
keetcheen=kitchen
kuma=bear
kuma no akachan=baby bear
kuma no mama=mama bear
kuma no papa=papa bear
nee=two
san=three
sanpo=stroll
teh-buru=table
ts'kareta=tired
ts'metai=cold
yawarakai=soft

The words in *green italics* throughout this fairy tale are words you've already learned in the previous level! Do you still remember what they mean?

from Cindellera (Level 1)

aishteru = in love
arigato = thank you
ashee = foot
chotto-no-aida = moment
doita-shimashteh = you're welcome
doresu = dress
eejeewaru = mean
hansamna = handsome
kanashee = sad
kawa-ee = pretty

kutsu = shoe
mahyonaka = midnight
ojisama = prince
okeena = big
oksan = wife
onanoko = girl
pahtee = party
sayonara = goodbye
shiawaseh = happy
yeh = house

1

kuma くま
kuma no papa くまのパパ
kuma no mama くまのママ

Once upon a time, there was a [bear] family that lived in a *yeh* in the forest – a [papa bear] who was extremely *okeena*, a very *kawa-ee* [mama bear], and their pride and joy, a cute

baby bear. The **kuma no akachan** was very little. The **cheesana kuma no akachan** was also very *hansamna* like the *okeena* **kuma no papa**. They were proud of their **kuma** family.

kuma no akachan
くまのあかちゃん

cheesana
ちいさな

3

One day, the **kuma no mama** prepared some soup for the **kuma no papa** and the **cheesana kuma no akachan**, but it was too hot. While it cooled off, the **kuma** family went for a [stroll].

sanpo
さんぽ

Meanwhile in a town nearby, there lived an *onanoko*, who was very *kawa-ee*, named Goldilocks. She was very *kanashee* because she never had anything fun to do.

She thought for a **chotto-no-aida** and decided to take a **sanpo** in the forest. Very soon, she came upon a **yeh** and knocked on the door but no one was there.

doa
ドア

So she opened the **doa**, put one *ashi* inside the *yeh*, and said "Hello? Is anyone home?" She was very tired after her long **sanpo** and since no one answered,

ts'kareta
つかれた

7

teh-buru
テーブル

keetcheen
キッチン

she walked slowly inside the *yeh*. She looked around the *yeh* and was very *shiawaseh* to see a an *okeena* table in the kitchen with bowls of food on it!

She quickly approached the *okeena* **teh-buru** in the **keetcheen** and was super extra *shiawaseh* because there on the **teh-buru** in the **keetcheen** was a bowl —

bo'oru
ボウル

eechee いち
nee に
san さん

but not just one **bo'oru**. There were one, two, three of them! **Eechee, nee, san** sitting on the **okeena teh-buru** in the **keetcheen**. She took a taste from the **okeena bo'oru** that belonged to

the **kuma no papa** and said, "This is too hot!"
Then she took a taste from the **bo'oru** that
belonged to the **kuma no mama** and said,
"This is too cold!" Then she took a taste from

atsui
あつい

ts'metai
つめたい

11

the **cheesana bo'oru** of the **cheesana kuma no akachan** and said, "Ah. This one isn't too **atsui**. It isn't too **ts'metai**. It's just right!" The **bo'oru** was very **cheesana** and she ate

everything in it. Well, now she was even more **ts'kareta** than ever after eating so much. So, she decided to rest. In the living room, she saw a chair ...but not just one **eesu**.

eesu
いす

There were **eechee**, **nee**, **san** of them! **Eechee, nee, san**! So, she sat down in the *okeena* **eesu** of the **kuma no papa** and said, "Oh! This **eesu** is too hard!"

katai
かたい

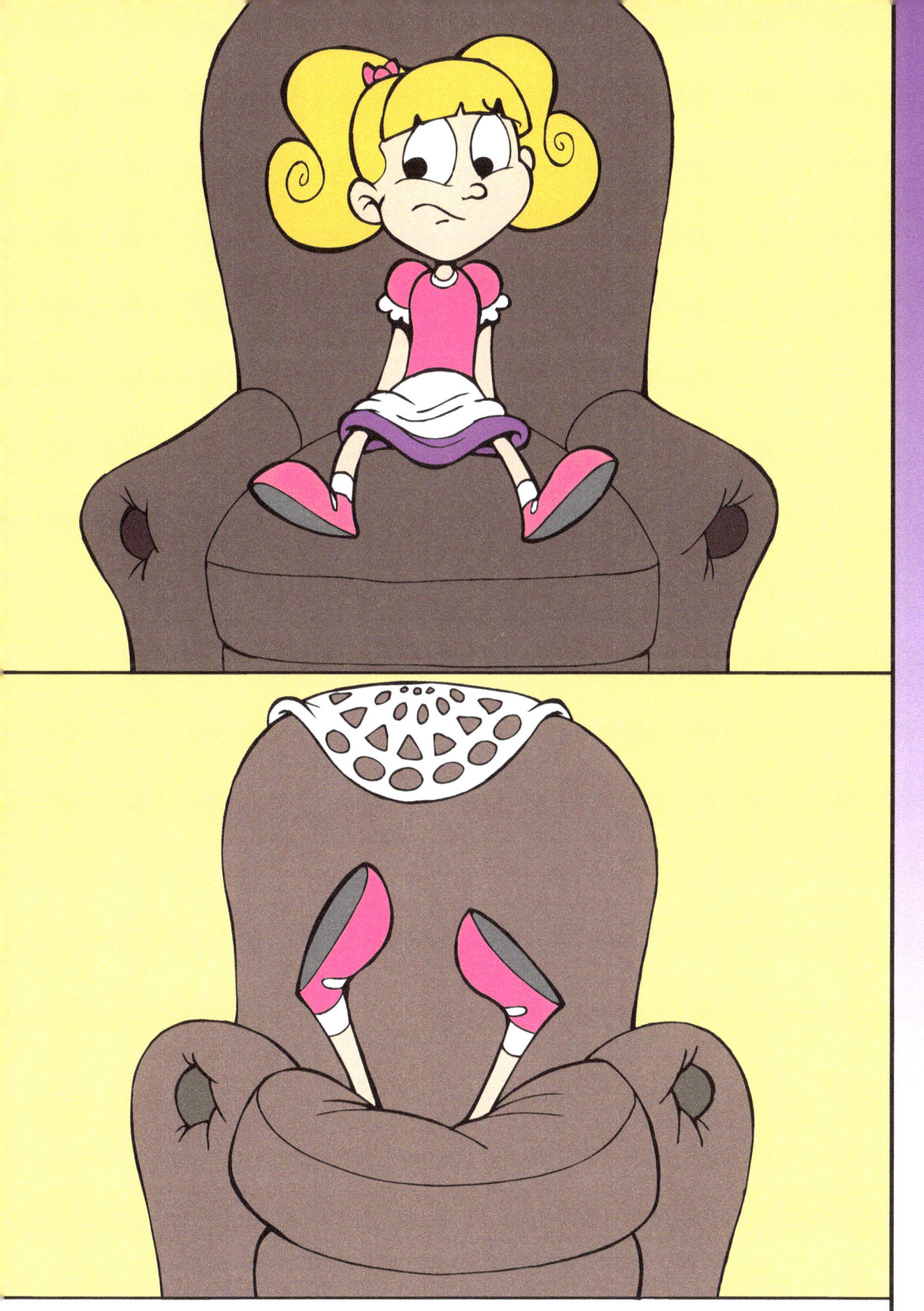

So, she sat in the **eesu** of the **kuma no mama** and said, "Oh! This **eesu** is too soft!" Then she sat in the **cheesana eesu** of the **cheesana kuma no akachan** and said,

yawarakai
やわらかい

15

"Ah. This **cheesana eesu** isn't too **katai**. It isn't too **yawarakai**. It's just right!"

But just as she got comfortable... *Crack!*

The **eesu** broke and completely fell apart!

Still **ts'kareta**, she decided to look for the bedroom to take a nap. In front of her, she saw a [bed]... but not just one **beddo**. There were **eechee**, **nee**, **san** of them!

beddo
ベッド

Eechee, **nee**, **san**! So, she tried the *okeena* **beddo** of the **kuma no papa**, but it was too **katai**. Then she tried the **beddo** of the **kuma no mama**, but it was too **yawarakai**. Finally,

she tried the **beddo** of the **cheesana kuma no akachan** and said, "Ah. This **beddo** isn't too **katai**. It isn't too **yawarakai**. It's just right!" And she fell asleep. At that very *chotto-no-aida*, the **kuma** family returned from their **sanpo**. As they walked in the **keecheen**, the *okeena* **kuma no papa** noticed something strange. "Someone's been eating my soup!" growled the *okeena*

kuma no papa. "And someone's been eating my soup!" said the **kuma no mama**. "And someone's been eating MY soup and ate it all up!" cried the **cheesana kuma no akachan**.

"Look!" said the **okeena kuma no papa**. "Someone's been sitting in my **eesu**!"

"And someone's been sitting in my **eesu**, as well!" said the **kuma no mama**.

"And someone's been sitting in my **eesu** and broke it into pieces!" cried the **cheesana kuma no akachan**. Then, the **kuma no papa**, the **kuma no mama**, and the **cheesana**

kuma no akachan heard snoring coming from the bedroom, so they went in to look. "Someone's been sleeping in my **beddo**!" said the *okeena* **kuma no papa**. "And someone's been

sleeping in my **beddo**," said the **kuma no mama**. "And someone's been sleeping in my **cheesana beddo** and there she is!" shouted the **cheesana kuma no akachan**.

25

Just then, Goldilocks woke up and was very surprised to see the **kuma** family! The **kuma** family thought the **cheesana** *onanoko* was very *eejeewaru* to use their *yeh*

without permission! "Oh, *arigato!*" Goldilocks said to the **kuma no papa**. "*Arigato* for letting me eat food from your **bo'oru**, sit in your **eesu**, and lie in your **beddo**. *Arigato!*" she said again,

expecting the **kuma** family to say, "*doita-shimashteh*!" but they were angry that she caused so much trouble in their **yeh** and the **kuma** family growled at her. So, she slowly

stood up on the **cheesana beddo** of the **cheesana kuma no akachan**, and nervously said, "Well, *arigato* for having me and… *sayonara!*" And with that, Goldilocks

29

jumped off the **cheesana beddo**, and dashed out the front **doa**, running as fast as each *ashi* could move. Needless to say, she never returned to visit the *yeh* of the **kuma** family again.

Now you're ready for Level 3!

Level 3 contains words from Levels 1 & 2, plus all NEW words!

For more HEY WORDY! products, visit...